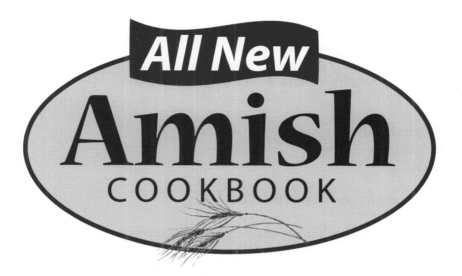

All New Amish COOKBOOK

pil

Publications International, Ltd.

Pictured on the front cover *(clockwise from top left):* Rosemary Chicken & Roasted Vegetables *(page 46),* Smothered Patties with Onion au Jus *(page 56),* Grandma's Favorite Sugarcakes *(page 78)* and Easy Shepherd's Pie *(page 42).*
Pictured on the back cover *(clockwise from top left):* Smoked Sausage and Cabbage *(page 36),* Brunswick Stew *(page 30)* and Orange Cinnamon Rolls *(page 6).*

ISBN-13: 978-1-4508-0131-7
ISBN-10: 1-4508-0131-5

Manufactured in China.

8 7 6 5 4 3 2 1

Microwave Cooking: Microwave ovens vary in wattage. Use the cooking times as guidelines and check for doneness before adding more time.

Preparation/Cooking Times: Preparation times are based on the approximate amount of time required to assemble the recipe before cooking, baking, chilling or serving. These times include preparation steps such as measuring, chopping and mixing. The fact that some preparations and cooking can be done simultaneously is taken into account. Preparation of optional ingredients and serving suggestions is not included.

Publications International, Ltd.

Table of Contents

Bread
Basket Bounty

Orange Cinnamon Rolls

½ cup packed brown sugar
3 tablespoons butter, melted, divided
1 tablespoon ground cinnamon
1 teaspoon grated orange peel
1 loaf (1 pound) frozen bread dough, thawed
⅓ cup raisins (optional)
½ cup powdered sugar, sifted
1 to 2 tablespoons orange juice

1. Grease 2 (8-inch) round cake pans. Combine brown sugar, 1 tablespoon butter, cinnamon and orange peel in small bowl; mix well.

2. Roll out dough on lightly floured surface to 18×8-inch rectangle. Brush dough with remaining 2 tablespoons butter; spread evenly with brown sugar mixture. Sprinkle with raisins, if desired. Starting with long side, roll up dough jelly-roll style; pinch seam to seal. Cut crosswise into 1-inch slices; arrange slices cut sides down in prepared pans. Cover loosely with plastic wrap. Let rise in warm place 30 to 40 minutes or until almost doubled in bulk.

3. Preheat oven to 350°F. Bake 18 minutes or until golden brown. Immediately remove to wire racks; cool slightly.

4. Whisk powdered sugar and orange juice in small bowl until smooth and consistency is thin enough to pour. Drizzle glaze over warm rolls.   *Makes 18 rolls*

Fruit and Nut Loaf

1½ cups plus 1 tablespoon all-purpose flour, divided
¾ cup mixed dried fruit
¼ cup chopped pecans
½ cup whole wheat flour
¼ cup sugar
1 tablespoon baking powder
¾ teaspoon baking soda
¼ teaspoon salt
3 eggs
¾ cup orange juice
¼ cup canola oil
¼ cup water
1 tablespoon grated orange peel
½ teaspoon vanilla

1. Preheat oven to 350°F. Lightly coat 8×4-inch loaf pan with nonstick cooking spray.

2. Combine 1 tablespoon all-purpose flour, dried fruit and pecans in small bowl; mix well.

3. Combine remaining 1½ cups all-purpose flour, whole wheat flour, sugar, baking powder, baking soda and salt in large bowl.

4. Whisk eggs, orange juice, oil, water, orange peel and vanilla in medium bowl until well blended. Gradually add to flour mixture; stir just until moistened. Stir in fruit mixture. Transfer to prepared pan.

5. Bake 35 to 40 minutes or until toothpick inserted into center comes out clean. Cool in pan 10 minutes. Remove to wire rack; cool completely.   *Makes 12 servings*

Fruit and Nut Loaf

Applesauce Muffins

1½ cups all-purpose flour
1 teaspoon *each* baking soda and ground cinnamon
½ teaspoon salt
¾ cup sugar
¾ cup applesauce
¼ cup (½ stick) butter, melted
1 egg
¾ cup *each* raisins and walnuts

1. Preheat oven to 350°F. Coat 12 standard (2½-inch) muffin cups with nonstick cooking spray.

2. Combine flour, baking soda, cinnamon and salt in large bowl. Add sugar, applesauce, butter and egg; mix well. Add raisins and walnuts; mix well. Divide batter among muffin cups.

3. Bake 18 to 20 minutes or until toothpick inserted into centers comes out clean. Cool in pan 5 minutes. Remove to wire rack; cool completely.   *Makes 12 muffins*

Grandma's Potato Biscuits

1 cup skim milk
3 tablespoons shortening
4 to 4½ cups all-purpose flour
1 tablespoon sugar
2¼ teaspoons active dry yeast
1½ teaspoons salt
1 cup mashed potatoes
2 eggs, beaten

Heat milk and shortening to 120°F. Stir together flour, sugar, yeast and salt. Combine with milk mixture, potatoes and eggs in bowl of electric stand mixer. Knead with dough hook until dough leaves side of bowl, 8 to 10 minutes. Cover and refrigerate at least 2 hours.

Roll dough to ½-inch thickness. Cut with 2½-inch cutter and place on pans coated with nonstick spray. Let rise until doubled. Bake at 400°F for 11 to 13 minutes.
Makes about 20 biscuits

Favorite recipe from *North Dakota Wheat Commission*

Bread Basket Bounty

Applesauce Muffins

Basic Cream Scones

2¼ cups all-purpose flour
¼ cup granulated sugar
1 tablespoon baking powder
½ teaspoon salt
6 tablespoons cold unsalted butter, cut into pieces
⅔ cup whipping cream
2 eggs, beaten
Coarse white decorating sugar

1. Preheat oven to 425°F. Combine flour, granulated sugar, baking powder and salt in food processor. Process using on/off pulsing action until blended. Add butter; process using on/off pulsing action until mixture resembles coarse crumbs. Transfer to large bowl.

2. Combine cream and eggs in small bowl; reserve 1 tablespoon egg mixture. Pour remaining egg mixture over flour mixture. Stir just until moistened.

3. Transfer dough to lightly floured surface. Shape into ball; pat into 8-inch disc. Cut into 8 wedges; place 2 inches apart on ungreased baking sheet. Brush reserved egg mixture over tops; sprinkle with coarse sugar.

4. Bake 12 to 14 minutes or until golden. Remove to wire rack; cool completely.

Makes 8 servings

Chocolate Chunk Scones: Stir ½ cup coarsely chopped semisweet chocolate into dough before shaping.

Ginger Peach Scones: Stir ⅓ cup chopped dried peaches and 1 tablespoon finely chopped crystallized ginger into dough before shaping.

Lemon Poppy Seed Scones: Stir grated peel of 1 lemon (about 3½ teaspoons) and 1 tablespoon poppy seeds into dough before shaping. Omit coarse sugar topping. Combine 1 cup powdered sugar and 2 tablespoons lemon juice (add up to 1½ teaspoons more lemon juice, if necessary, for desired consistency) in small bowl. Drizzle over slightly cooled scones.

Maple Pecan Scones: Stir ½ cup coarsely chopped pecans into dough before shaping. Omit coarse sugar topping. Combine ¾ cup powdered sugar and 2 tablespoons maple syrup in small bowl. Drizzle over slightly cooled scones.

13

Maple Pecan, Chocolate Chunk, Ginger Peach
and Lemon Poppy Seed Scones

Sugar-and-Spice Twists

2 tablespoons sugar
½ teaspoon ground cinnamon
1 package (11 ounces) refrigerated breadstick dough (12 breadsticks)

1. Preheat oven to 350°F. Lightly coat baking sheet with nonstick cooking spray.

2. Combine sugar and cinnamon in shallow dish or plate. Divide dough into 12 pieces. Roll each piece into 12-inch rope. Roll in cinnamon-sugar. Twist into pretzel shape. Place on prepared baking sheet.

3. Bake 15 to 18 minutes or until lightly browned. Remove to wire rack; cool 5 minutes. Serve warm.   *Makes 12 servings*

Baking Powder Biscuits

2¼ cups all-purpose flour
1 tablespoon baking powder
½ teaspoon salt
¼ cup (½ stick) cold butter, cut into 4 pieces
¾ cup milk

1. Preheat oven to 450°F. Combine flour, baking powder and salt in food processor. Process using on/off pulsing action until blended. Add butter; process until mixture resembles coarse crumbs. Pour in milk. Process using on/off pulsing action just until blended and dough is soft.

2. Transfer dough to lightly floured surface. Knead gently 6 to 8 times. Roll out or pat dough into ½-inch-thick circle.

3. Cut dough into 2½-inch circles using floured cutter. Place biscuits on ungreased cookie sheet. Bake 12 to 15 minutes or until golden. Serve immediately.

Makes 1 dozen biscuits

Sugar-and-Spice Twists

Crunchy Whole Grain Bread

2 cups warm water (105°F to 115°F), divided
⅓ cup honey
2 tablespoons vegetable oil
1 tablespoon salt
2 packages (4½ teaspoons) active dry yeast
½ cup water
2 to 2½ cups whole wheat flour, divided
1 cup bread flour
1¼ cup quick oats, divided
½ cup hulled pumpkin seeds or sunflower kernels
½ cup assorted grains and seeds
1 egg white
1 tablespoon water

1. Combine 1½ cups water, honey, oil and salt in medium saucepan. Cook and stir over low heat until warm (115°F to 120°F).

2. Dissolve yeast in remaining ½ cup water in bowl of electric stand mixer. Let stand 5 minutes. Stir in honey mixture. Add 1 cup whole wheat flour and bread flour. With dough hook, mix at low speed 2 minutes or until combined. Gradually stir in 1 cup oats, pumpkin seeds and assorted grains. Add remaining whole wheat flour, ½ cup at a time, just until dough begins to form a ball. Continue mixing 7 to 10 minutes or until dough is smooth and elastic.

3. Place dough in lightly oiled bowl, turning to coat top. Cover loosely with plastic wrap. Let rise in warm place 1½ to 2 hours or until doubled in bulk.

4. Grease 2 (9×5-inch) loaf pans. Punch down dough. Divide in half. Shape each half into loaf; place in prepared loaf pans. Cover with plastic wrap. Let rise in warm place 1 hour or until almost doubled in bulk.

5. Preheat oven to 375°F. Whisk egg white and water in small bowl. Brush tops of loaves with egg mixture. Sprinkle with remaining ¼ cup oats. Bake 35 to 45 minutes or until loaves sound hollow when tapped. Cool in pans 10 minutes. Remove to wire rack; cool completely.

Makes 2 loaves

Crunchy Whole Grain Bread

Apple-Cheddar Muffins

1 cup whole wheat flour
1 cup all-purpose white flour
2 tablespoons sugar
1 tablespoon baking powder
½ teaspoon salt
1 cup peeled chopped apple
1 cup grated CABOT® Mild or Sharp Cheddar
2 large eggs
1 cup milk
4 tablespoons CABOT® Salted Butter, melted

1. Preheat oven to 400°F. Butter 12 muffin cups or coat with nonstick cooking spray.

2. In mixing bowl, stir together whole wheat and white flour, sugar, baking powder and salt. Add apple and cheese and toss to combine.

3. In another bowl, whisk eggs lightly. Whisk in milk and butter. Make well in center of dry ingredients; add milk mixture and gently stir in dry ingredients from side until just combined.

4. Divide batter among prepared muffin cups. Bake for 20 minutes or until muffins feel firm when lightly pressed on top.   *Makes 12 muffins*

Milled from the entire wheat kernel, whole wheat flour retains all of the grain's natural flavor, color and nutrients. It is generally used in combination with all-purpose or bread flour to avoid overly dense or poorly risen loaves.

Apple-Cheddar Muffins

Cinnamon Raisin Bread

4 cups all-purpose flour
2½ teaspoons salt
2½ teaspoons active dry yeast
¼ cup (½ stick) butter
1 cup plus 2 tablespoons milk
2 tablespoons honey
2 eggs
1 cup raisins
2 tablespoons melted butter, divided
8 teaspoons sugar
4 teaspoons ground cinnamon

1. Combine flour, salt and yeast in bowl of electric stand mixer. Melt ¼ cup butter in small saucepan over low heat; stir in milk and honey until mixture is warm (115°F to 120°F). Whisk in eggs; remove from heat.

2. Add egg mixture and raisins to flour mixture. With dough hook, mix on low speed until dough separates from sides of bowl and forms a ball. Continue mixing 2 minutes.

3. Place dough in lightly oiled bowl, turning to coat top. Cover loosely with plastic wrap. Let rise in warm place 1 to 1½ hours or until doubled in bulk.

4. Grease and flour 2 (8×4-inch) loaf pans. Punch down dough. Divide in half. Shape each half into 8×10-inch rectangle. Brush tops of dough with 1 tablespoon melted butter.

5. Combine sugar and cinnamon in small bowl. Reserve 2 teaspoons cinnamon-sugar; sprinkle remaining cinnamon-sugar evenly over dough.

6. Roll up 1 dough rectangle, starting with short side; place in prepared loaf pan. Repeat with remaining dough. Cover with plastic wrap. Let rise in warm place 1 to 1½ hours or until almost doubled in bulk.

7. Preheat oven to 375°F. Bake 35 minutes or until golden brown (internal temperature should register 180°F), rotating pans once. Brush tops with remaining 1 tablespoon melted butter; sprinkle with reserved cinnamon-sugar. Cool in pans 10 minutes. Remove to wire rack; cool completely.

Makes 2 loaves

Cinnamon Raisin Bread

Dutch Oven Stews

Old-Fashioned Beef Stew

1½ pounds beef top or bottom round steak
3 teaspoons olive oil, divided
4 cups sliced mushrooms
2 cloves garlic, minced
2 cups baby carrots
2 cups beef broth
2 tablespoons tomato paste
¾ teaspoon dried thyme
½ teaspoon salt
½ teaspoon black pepper
2 bay leaves
2 onions, cut into wedges
2 cups frozen cut green beans
3 tablespoons water
3 tablespoons all-purpose flour

1. Cut beef into 1-inch cubes. Heat 2 teaspoons oil in Dutch oven over medium-high heat. Brown beef in batches; transfer to plate.

2. Heat remaining 1 teaspoon oil in same Dutch oven. Add mushrooms; cook and stir until browned. Add garlic; cook and stir 30 seconds. Add beef, carrots, broth, tomato paste, thyme, salt, pepper and bay leaves. Bring to a boil over medium-high heat. Reduce heat to low; cover and simmer 2 hours or until beef is fork-tender. Add onions and green beans during last 30 minutes of cooking.

3. Remove and discard bay leaves. Stir water into flour in small bowl until smooth. Stir into stew; simmer 2 to 3 minutes or until thickened. *Makes 6 servings*

Chicken and Herb Stew

½ cup all-purpose flour
½ teaspoon salt
¼ teaspoon black pepper
¼ teaspoon paprika
4 chicken drumsticks
4 chicken thighs
2 tablespoons olive oil
12 ounces new potatoes, quartered
2 carrots, quartered lengthwise and cut into 3-inch pieces
1 green bell pepper, cut into thin strips
¾ cup chopped onion
2 cloves garlic, minced
1¾ cups water
¼ cup dry white wine
2 chicken bouillon cubes
1 tablespoon chopped fresh oregano
1 teaspoon chopped fresh rosemary leaves
2 tablespoons chopped fresh Italian parsley (optional)

1. Combine flour, salt, black pepper and paprika in shallow dish; stir until well blended. Coat chicken pieces with flour mixture; shake off excess.

2. Heat oil in Dutch oven over medium-high heat. Add chicken; cook 8 minutes or until brown on both sides, turning once. Transfer to plate.

3. Add potatoes, carrots, bell pepper, onion and garlic to same Dutch oven; cook and stir 5 minutes or until lightly browned. Add water, wine and bouillon; cook 1 minute, stirring to scrape up browned bits. Add oregano and rosemary.

4. Arrange chicken on top of vegetable mixture, turning several times to coat. Reduce heat to medium-low; cover and simmer 45 to 50 minutes or until chicken is cooked through (165°F), turning occasionally. Sprinkle with parsley, if desired.

Makes 4 servings

Chicken and Herb Stew

Hearty Vegetable Stew

1 tablespoon olive oil
1 cup chopped onion
¾ cup chopped carrots
3 cloves garlic, minced
4 cups coarsely chopped green cabbage
3½ cups coarsely chopped unpeeled new red potatoes
1 teaspoon salt
1 teaspoon dried rosemary
½ teaspoon black pepper
4 cups vegetable broth
1 can (about 15 ounces) Great Northern beans, rinsed and drained
1 can (about 14 ounces) diced tomatoes

1. Heat oil in Dutch oven over medium-high heat. Add onion and carrots; cook and stir 3 minutes. Add garlic; cook and stir 1 minute.

2. Add cabbage, potatoes, salt, rosemary and pepper; cook 1 minute. Stir in broth, beans and tomatoes; bring to a boil. Reduce heat to medium-low; simmer 15 minutes or until potatoes are tender. *Makes 6 to 8 servings*

Sausage Stew

1 pound BOB EVANS® Italian Sausage Roll
2 cans (14½ ounces each) Italian-style diced tomatoes
2 cans (14½ ounces each) beef broth
1 can (16 ounces) red kidney beans, drained and rinsed
1 bag (16 ounces) frozen Italian blend vegetables
1 bag (8 ounces) egg noodles

In a Dutch oven, crumble and cook sausage over medium heat until browned; drain. Add tomatoes, beef broth, beans, frozen vegetables and noodles. Bring to a boil. Stir and reduce heat to low. Cook 7 to 10 minutes or until vegetables and noodles are tender, stirring occasionally. *Makes 4 to 6 servings*

Hearty Vegetable Stew

Baked Bean Stew

    1 cup chopped onion
    1 cup chopped green pepper
    1 tablespoon vegetable oil
 12 ounces boneless skinless chicken breast or tenders, cut into
        ½-inch pieces
    2 cans (15 ounces each) baked beans or pork and beans
    1 can (15 ounces) garbanzo beans or black-eyes *or* 1½ cups cooked
        dry-packaged garbanzo beans or black-eyes, rinsed, drained
    1 can (14½ ounces) diced tomatoes with roasted garlic, undrained
    ¾ teaspoon dried sage leaves
    ½ teaspoon ground cumin
      Salt and black pepper

1. Cook onion and green pepper in oil in large saucepan over medium heat until tender, 3 to 4 minutes. Add chicken and cook until browned, 3 to 4 minutes.

2. Add beans, tomatoes, sage and cumin to saucepan; heat to boiling. Reduce heat and simmer, uncovered, 8 to 10 minutes. Season to taste with salt and black pepper.

Makes 8 servings

Favorite recipe from ***American Dry Bean Board***

If you're in a hurry, you can use a frozen chopped onion and green pepper blend. You can also plan ahead, as the stew can be prepared and refrigerated 1 to 2 days in advance or frozen for up to 2 months.

Baked Bean Stew

Brunswick Stew

1 whole chicken (about 4 pounds), cut up
2 quarts water
1 stalk celery (including leaves), cut into 2-inch pieces
1 onion, quartered
1 clove garlic, halved
2 teaspoons salt
1 teaspoon whole black peppercorns
1 can (about 14 ounces) diced tomatoes
2 russet potatoes, peeled and cubed
1 onion, thinly sliced
¼ cup tomato paste
1 teaspoon sugar
½ teaspoon ground black pepper
½ teaspoon dried thyme
⅛ teaspoon garlic powder
    Dash hot pepper sauce
1 package (10 ounces) frozen lima beans
1 package (10 ounces) frozen corn

1. Place chicken and water in Dutch oven; bring to a boil over medium-high heat. Skim off foam. Add celery, quartered onion, garlic, salt and peppercorns; return to a boil. Reduce heat to medium-low; cover and simmer 2½ to 3 hours or until thighs are cooked through.

2. Remove chicken from broth; cool slightly. Remove meat, discarding skin and bones. Cut enough chicken into 1-inch pieces to measure 3 cups. (Reserve remaining chicken for another use.)

3. Strain and reserve broth through double thickness of cheesecloth. Discard vegetables; skim off fat. Return 1 quart broth to Dutch oven. (Reserve remaining broth for another use.)

4. Add tomatoes, potatoes, sliced onion, tomato paste, sugar, ground pepper, thyme, garlic powder and hot pepper sauce. Bring to a boil over medium-high heat. Reduce heat to medium-low; cover and simmer 30 minutes.

5. Add lima beans and corn; simmer, covered, 5 minutes. Add chicken; cook 5 minutes or until heated through. *Makes 6 to 8 servings*

Brunswick Stew

Hearty One-Pot Chicken Stew

12 *Tyson*® Individually Frozen Boneless Skinless Chicken Tenderloins
1 box traditional red beans and rice mix
2¼ cups water
1 can (14.5 ounces) diced tomatoes, undrained
3 new red potatoes, unpeeled, cut into 1-inch pieces
2 carrots, sliced ½ inch thick
1 onion, cut into 1-inch pieces

1. Wash hands. Remove protective ice glaze from frozen chicken by holding under cool running water 1 to 2 minutes. Cut into 1-inch pieces. Wash hands.

2. In large saucepan, combine chicken, beans and rice, contents of seasoning packet, water, tomatoes, potatoes, carrots and onion. Bring to a boil. Cover, reduce heat; simmer 20 minutes or until internal juices of chicken run clear. (Or insert instant-read meat thermometer into thickest part of chicken. Temperature should read 180°F.) Refrigerate leftovers immediately. *Makes 4 servings*

Dijon Lamb Stew

½ pound boneless lamb, cut into small pieces*
½ medium onion, chopped
½ teaspoon dried rosemary
1 tablespoon olive oil
1 can (14½ ounces) DEL MONTE® Original Recipe Stewed Tomatoes
1 carrot, julienne cut
1 tablespoon Dijon mustard
1 can (15 ounces) white beans or pinto beans, drained

Beef top sirloin steak can be substituted for lamb.

1. Brown meat with onion and rosemary in oil in large skillet over medium-high heat, stirring occasionally. Season with salt and pepper, if desired.

2. Add undrained tomatoes, carrot and mustard. Cover and cook over medium heat 10 minutes; add beans.

3. Cook, uncovered, over medium heat 5 minutes, stirring occasionally. Garnish with sliced ripe olives and chopped parsley, if desired. *Makes 4 servings*

Dutch Oven Stews

Hearty One-Pot Chicken Stew

Thyme for Chicken Stew with Polenta Dumplings

4 tablespoons olive oil, divided
2 pounds boneless skinless chicken thighs
2 medium eggplants, chopped
6 onions, chopped
4 tomatoes, seeded and diced
1 cup chicken broth
⅓ cup pitted black olives, sliced
1 tablespoon chopped fresh thyme *or* 1 teaspoon dried thyme
1 tablespoon red wine vinegar
Polenta Dumplings (recipe follows)

1. Preheat oven to 350°F. Heat 1 tablespoon oil in Dutch oven over medium-high heat. Cook chicken in batches 5 minutes or until brown on both sides, turning once. Transfer to plate.

2. Heat remaining 3 tablespoons oil in same Dutch oven; add eggplants, onions and tomatoes. Reduce heat to medium. Cook and stir 5 minutes. Return chicken to Dutch oven. Stir in broth, olives, thyme and vinegar. Bring to a boil; cover. Transfer to oven and bake 1 hour. Meanwhile, prepare Polenta Dumplings.

3. Top stew with rounded tablespoonfuls dumpling mixture. Bake, uncovered, 20 minutes or until dumplings are cooked through.   *Makes 6 servings*

Polenta Dumplings: Bring 3½ cups chicken broth to a boil in medium saucepan over medium-high heat. Gradually whisk in 1 cup polenta. Reduce heat to low; simmer 15 minutes or until thickened, stirring constantly. Remove from heat; stir in ½ cup grated Parmesan cheese, ¼ cup chopped fresh Italian parsley, 1 beaten egg and 2 tablespoons butter.

Spiced Pork and Apple Stew

1 tablespoon canola oil

1¼ pounds pork stew meat, cut into 1-inch pieces

1 onion, cut into ½-inch-thick slices

2 cloves garlic, minced

1 can (28 ounces) crushed tomatoes

1 cup chicken broth

2 tablespoons spicy brown mustard

1 tablespoon brown sugar

2 teaspoons ground cinnamon

1 teaspoon ground cumin

¼ teaspoon salt

3 red potatoes, cut into 1-inch pieces (about 3 cups)

1½ cups baby carrots

2 apples, cored and cubed

1. Heat oil in Dutch oven over medium-high heat. Brown pork in batches. Add onion and garlic. Reduce heat to medium. Cover; cook and stir 5 minutes.

2. Stir in tomatoes, broth, mustard, brown sugar, cinnamon, cumin and salt. Bring to a boil. Reduce heat to medium-low; cover and simmer 30 minutes.

3. Stir in potatoes, carrots and apples; simmer, covered, 45 minutes or until pork and vegetables are tender. *Makes 6 to 8 servings*

If your grocery store does not have pork stew meat available, you can purchase an equal amount of boneless pork shoulder or pork loin and simply cut it into 1- to 2-inch cubes yourself.

Dutch Oven Stews

Satisfying
Suppers

Smoked Sausage and Cabbage

1 pound smoked sausage, cut into 2-inch pieces
1 tablespoon olive oil
6 cups coarsely chopped cabbage
1 yellow onion, cut into ½-inch wedges
2 cloves garlic, minced
¾ teaspoon sugar
¼ teaspoon caraway seeds
¼ teaspoon salt
¼ teaspoon black pepper
1 package (2 pounds) refrigerated mashed potatoes

1. Heat large nonstick skillet over medium-high heat. Add sausage; cook and stir 3 minutes or until browned. Transfer to plate.

2. Heat oil in same skillet. Add cabbage, onion, garlic, sugar, caraway seeds, salt and pepper; cook and stir 5 minutes or until onion begins to brown. Add sausage; cover and cook 5 minutes. Remove from heat. Let stand 5 minutes.

3. Meanwhile, heat potatoes in microwave according to package directions. Serve sausage mixture over mashed potatoes. *Makes 4 servings*

Cheese-Filled Chicken Roll-Ups

4 *Tyson*® Individually Frozen Boneless Skinless Chicken Breasts, thoroughly thawed
4 ounces herbed or plain soft goat cheese (chèvre)
1 cup shredded sharp Cheddar cheese
1 egg
½ cup seasoned bread crumbs

1. Preheat oven to 375°F. Wash hands. Spray 9-inch square baking pan with nonstick cooking spray. In small bowl, mix goat cheese and Cheddar with fork until blended.

2. Place chicken breasts between 2 layers of plastic wrap or waxed paper. With rolling pin or flat meat mallet, pound to flatten slightly. Spread one-fourth of cheese mixture on each chicken breast. Starting at short end, roll up breast and tuck ends to enclose filling. Secure with wooden picks, if desired.

3. In shallow dish, blend egg and 1 tablespoon water. Place bread crumbs on waxed paper or in shallow dish. Coat chicken evenly with egg mixture, then coat well (including ends) with bread crumbs. Place in baking pan. Spray chicken lightly with nonstick cooking spray to moisten coating. Wash hands.

4. Bake 25 to 30 minutes or until internal juices of chicken run clear. (Or insert instant-read meat thermometer into thickest part of chicken. Temperature should read 180°F.) Let stand 5 minutes before serving. Refrigerate leftovers immediately.

Makes 4 servings

Prep Time: 20 minutes • **Cook Time:** 30 minutes

Cheese-Filled Chicken Roll-Ups

Browned Pork Chops with Gravy

½ teaspoon dried sage
½ teaspoon dried marjoram
¼ teaspoon black pepper
⅛ teaspoon salt
4 boneless pork loin chops
　Olive oil cooking spray
¼ cup chopped onion
1 clove garlic, minced
1 cup sliced mushrooms
¾ cup beef broth
⅓ cup sour cream
1 tablespoon all-purpose flour
1 teaspoon Dijon mustard
2 cups hot cooked wide egg noodles
　Chopped fresh Italian parsley (optional)

1. Combine sage, marjoram, pepper and salt in small bowl. Rub onto both sides of pork chops. Spray large nonstick skillet with cooking spray; heat over medium heat. Add pork chops; cook 5 minutes or until barely pink in center, turning once. Transfer to plate; keep warm.

2. Add onion and garlic to same skillet; cook and stir 2 minutes. Add mushrooms and broth; bring to a boil. Reduce heat to medium-low; cover and simmer 3 to 4 minutes or until mushrooms are tender.

3. Whisk together sour cream, flour and mustard in medium bowl. Whisk in about 3 tablespoons broth mixture from skillet. Stir sour cream mixture into skillet. Cook and stir until mixture comes to a boil. Serve gravy over pork chops and noodles. Sprinkle with parsley, if desired.　　　　　　　　　　　　　　　　*Makes 4 servings*

Browned Pork Chop with Gravy

Meatloaf

1 pound lean ground beef
1 egg, beaten
½ cup CREAM OF WHEAT® Hot Cereal (Instant, 1-minute, 2½-minute or
    10-minute cook time), uncooked
¼ cup ketchup, divided
¼ cup finely chopped onion
2 tablespoons water
¾ teaspoon salt

1. Preheat oven to 350°F. Grease shallow baking dish.

2. Mix ground beef, egg, Cream of Wheat, 2 tablespoons ketchup, onion, water and salt in large bowl. Shape into loaf in prepared baking dish.

3. Bake 35 minutes. Spread remaining ketchup over meatloaf. Bake 15 minutes longer or until meat thermometer inserted into center reads 160°F.

Makes 4 servings

Easy Shepherd's Pie

1½ pounds lean ground beef
1 cup chopped onion
2 cups frozen green beans, thawed
1 cup frozen corn niblets, thawed
1 can (14.5 ounces) diced tomatoes, drained
1 jar (12 ounces) beef gravy
1 teaspoon dried thyme leaves
½ teaspoon salt
1 package SIMPLY POTATOES® Mashed Potatoes

1. Heat oven to 375°F. Spray 2½- to 3-quart casserole baking dish with nonstick cooking spray.

2. In 12-inch skillet cook ground beef and onion until browned; drain grease. Add beans, corn, tomatoes, gravy, thyme and salt. Cook until heated through. Spoon beef mixture into casserole dish. Spread **Simply Potatoes®** evenly over beef mixture. Bake 30 to 35 minutes or until edges are bubbly. Remove from oven.

3. Heat broiler. Broil casserole 4 to 6 inches from heat, 3 to 5 minutes, until **Simply Potatoes®** are lightly browned.

Makes 6 servings

Satisfying Suppers

Seared Spiced Pork Tenderloin and Apples

½ teaspoon ground cinnamon
½ teaspoon ground cumin
½ teaspoon black pepper
¼ teaspoon salt
⅛ teaspoon ground allspice
1 pound pork tenderloin
1 teaspoon canola oil
2 medium Fuji or Gala apples, sliced
¼ cup water
¼ cup raisins
1 tablespoon butter

1. Preheat oven to 425°F. Line baking sheet with foil. Combine cinnamon, cumin, pepper, salt and allspice in small bowl; mix well. Sprinkle evenly over all sides of pork, pressing to adhere.

2. Heat oil in large skillet over medium-high heat. Add pork; cook until brown on all sides, turning frequently. Transfer to prepared baking sheet.

3. Bake 18 minutes or until barely pink in center. Transfer pork to cutting board; let stand 5 minutes.

4. Add apples, water and raisins to skillet; cook and stir over medium-high heat 2 minutes or until apples begin to brown. Remove from heat; stir in butter. Cover and let stand until ready to serve. Thinly slice pork and serve with apple mixture.

Makes 2 to 4 servings

Seared Spiced Pork Tenderloin and Apples

Rosemary Chicken & Roasted Vegetables

1 (3-pound) whole broiler-fryer chicken

1 tablespoon butter, melted

4 medium red potatoes, cut into quarters

2 cups fresh or frozen whole baby carrots

2 stalks celery, cut into 2-inch pieces (about 1½ cups)

12 small white onions, peeled

1½ teaspoons chopped fresh rosemary leaves *or* ½ teaspoon dried rosemary leaves, crushed

1 cup SWANSON® Chicken Stock

½ cup orange juice

1. Brush the chicken with the butter. Place the chicken and vegetables into a roasting pan. Season with the rosemary. Stir the stock and orange juice in a small bowl and pour **half** the stock mixture over the chicken and vegetables.

2. Roast at 375°F. for 45 minutes.

3. Stir the vegetables. Add the remaining stock mixture to the pan. Roast for 30 minutes or until the chicken is cooked through.　　*Makes 4 servings*

Prep Time: 15 minutes • **Bake Time:** 1 hour, 15 minutes

To quickly peel the onions, place them in a medium bowl. Cover with boiling water. Let stand for 5 minutes. Drain and slip off the skins.

Rosemary Chicken & Roasted Vegetables

Yankee Pot Roast

1 boneless beef chuck pot roast (arm, shoulder or blade), about 2½ pounds
⅓ cup all-purpose flour
¾ teaspoon salt
¾ teaspoon pepper
1 tablespoon vegetable oil
1 can (14 to 14½ ounces) beef broth
½ cup dry red wine
1½ teaspoons dried thyme leaves, crushed
2 packages (16 ounces each) frozen stew vegetable mixture
    (such as potatoes, carrots, celery and onion)

1. Combine flour, salt and pepper. Lightly coat beef in 2 tablespoons of the flour mixture. Heat oil in large stockpot over medium heat until hot. Place beef pot roast in stockpot; brown evenly. Pour off drippings.

2. Combine beef broth, red wine, thyme and remaining flour mixture; add to stockpot and bring to a boil. Reduce heat; cover tightly and simmer 2 hours. Add vegetables to stockpot; continue simmering 30 to 45 minutes or until pot roast and vegetables are fork-tender.

3. Remove pot roast and vegetables; keep warm. Skim fat from cooking liquid, if necessary.

4. Cut pot roast into bite-size pieces. Serve with vegetables and gravy.

Makes 6 servings

Favorite recipe from ***Courtesy The Beef Checkoff***

Prep and Cook Time: 3 hours to 3½ hours

Yankee Pot Roast

Garlicky Oven-Fried Chicken Thighs

1 egg
2 tablespoons water
1 cup plain dry bread crumbs
1 teaspoon salt
1 teaspoon garlic powder
½ teaspoon black pepper
¼ teaspoon ground red pepper
8 chicken thighs (about 3 pounds)
   Olive oil cooking spray

1. Preheat oven to 350°F.

2. Beat egg with water in shallow bowl. Combine bread crumbs, salt, garlic powder, black pepper and red pepper in separate shallow bowl.

3. Dip chicken into egg mixture; turn to coat. Transfer to bread crumb mixture; press lightly to coat both sides. Place, skin side up, on large baking sheet.

4. Lightly spray chicken with cooking spray. Bake 50 to 60 minutes or until browned and cooked through (165°F). *Do not turn chicken during cooking.*   *Makes 4 servings*

Ham Pot Pie

1 (10¾-ounce) can condensed cream of broccoli soup, undiluted
⅓ cup milk
⅛ teaspoon dried thyme leaves
¼ teaspoon coarsely ground pepper
2 (5-ounce) cans HORMEL® chunk ham, drained and flaked
1 (10-ounce) package frozen vegetables, thawed and drained.
1 (4½-ounce) can refrigerated buttermilk biscuits (6 count)

Heat oven to 400°F. In 1½-quart round baking dish, combine soup, milk, thyme and pepper. Stir in ham and vegetables. Bake 20 to 25 minutes. Separate biscuits; cut each biscuit into quarters. Arrange biscuits over ham mixture. Bake 12 to 15 minutes longer or until biscuits are golden brown.   *Makes 6 servings*

Garlicky Oven-Fried Chicken Thighs

Pork and Corn Bread Stuffing Casserole

½ teaspoon paprika
¼ teaspoon salt
¼ teaspoon garlic powder
¼ teaspoon black pepper
4 bone-in pork chops
2 tablespoons butter
1½ cups chopped onions
¾ cup thinly sliced celery
¾ cup matchstick carrots*
¼ cup chopped fresh Italian parsley
1 can (about 14 ounces) chicken broth
4 cups corn bread stuffing mix

Matchstick carrots (sometimes called shredded carrots) can be found near other prepared vegetables in the supermarket produce section.

1. Preheat oven to 350°F. Lightly coat 13×9-inch baking dish with nonstick cooking spray.

2. Combine paprika, salt, garlic powder and pepper in small bowl. Sprinkle over both sides of pork chops.

3. Melt butter in large skillet over medium-high heat. Add pork chops; cook 4 minutes or just until browned, turning once. Transfer to plate.

4. Add onions, celery, carrots and parsley to same skillet. Cook and stir 4 minutes or until onions are translucent. Add broth; bring to a boil. Remove from heat; add stuffing mix and fluff with fork.

5. Transfer stuffing mixture to prepared baking dish. Top with pork chops. Cover; bake 25 minutes or until pork is barely pink in center.   *Makes 4 servings*

Variation: For a one-skillet meal, use an ovenproof skillet. Place browned pork chops on mixture in skillet; cover and bake as directed.

Pork and Corn Bread Stuffing Casserole

Classic Beef Stroganoff

1 cup MINUTE® White Rice, uncooked
1 tablespoon vegetable oil
1 cup onion, chopped
1 pound lean ground beef
2 cups mushrooms, sliced
1 can (14½ ounces) beef broth
1 can (10¾ ounces) cream of mushroom soup
1 tablespoon Worcestershire sauce
½ cup sour cream

Prepare rice according to package directions.

Heat oil in medium skillet over medium-high heat. Add onion; cook and stir 3 minutes. Add beef and brown; drain excess fat.

Add mushrooms, broth, soup and Worcestershire sauce. Bring to a boil and simmer 5 minutes. Stir in sour cream. Serve over rice.   *Makes 4 servings*

Chicken with White Beans

2 cans (10¾ ounces each) CAMPBELL'S® Condensed Tomato Soup
    (Regular or Healthy Request®)
1 teaspoon dried oregano leaves, crushed
¼ teaspoon garlic powder or 2 cloves garlic, minced
2 cans (about 16 ounces each) white kidney (cannellini) beans, rinsed and
    drained
1 large onion, chopped (about 1 cup)
4 skinless, boneless chicken breast halves

1. Stir the soup, oregano, garlic powder, beans and onion in an 11×8-inch (2-quart) shallow baking dish. Top with the chicken.

2. Bake at 400°F. for 50 minutes or until the chicken is cooked through. Stir the mixture before serving.   *Makes 4 servings*

Prep Time: 10 minutes • **Bake Time:** 50 minutes

Classic Beef Stroganoff

Smothered Patties with Onion au Jus

1 pound ground beef
⅛ teaspoon salt
   Nonstick cooking spray
1 onion, thinly sliced
¾ cup water
2 teaspoons beef bouillon granules
1 teaspoon Worcestershire sauce
½ teaspoon instant coffee granules
⅛ teaspoon black pepper

1. Shape beef into 4 patties about ½ inch thick. Sprinkle with salt.

2. Lightly coat large nonstick skillet with cooking spray; heat over medium-high heat. Add patties; cook 6 minutes or until just barely pink in center, turning once. Transfer to plate.

3. Lightly coat same skillet with cooking spray. Add onion; cook and stir 3 minutes or until tender. Transfer to plate.

4. Add water, bouillon, Worcestershire sauce, coffee and pepper to skillet; bring to a boil. Reduce heat to medium-low; simmer 3 minutes or until mixture is reduced to ½ cup.

5. Return the patties and onion to skillet. Turn patties several times to coat; cook 1 minute or until heated through.   *Makes 2 to 4 servings*

Smothered Patty with Onion au Jus

Vegetable *Variety*

Savory Mushroom Bread Pudding

Vegetable cooking spray
12 slices PEPPERIDGE FARM® White Sandwich Bread or PEPPERIDGE FARM® Whole Grain 100% Whole Wheat Bread, cut into cubes
1 package (8 ounces) sliced mushrooms
1 can (10¾ ounces) CAMPBELL'S® Condensed Cream of Mushroom Soup (Regular or 98% Fat Free)
4 eggs
2½ cups milk
1 teaspoon dried thyme leaves, crushed
⅛ teaspoon ground black pepper
1 cup shredded Swiss cheese (about 4 ounces)

1. Heat the oven to 375°F. Spray a 13×9-inch (3-quart) shallow baking dish with cooking spray.

2. Add the bread and mushrooms to prepared baking dish.

3. Beat the soup, eggs, milk, thyme and black pepper with a whisk or a fork in a medium bowl. Pour over the bread and mushrooms, pressing down the bread to coat. Let stand for 30 minutes.

4. Bake for 35 minutes. Top with the cheese. Bake for 10 minutes more or until the cheese melts. *Makes 6 servings*

Prep Time: 5 minutes • **Stand Time:** 30 minutes • **Bake Time:** 45 minutes

Chunky Ranch Potatoes

    3 pounds unpeeled red potatoes, quartered
    1 cup water
    ½ cup ranch dressing
    ½ cup grated Parmesan or Cheddar cheese (optional)
    ¼ cup minced chives

Slow Cooker Directions

1. Place potatoes and water in slow cooker. Cover; cook on LOW 7 to 9 hours or on HIGH 4 to 6 hours or until potatoes are tender.

2. Stir in ranch dressing, cheese, if desired, and chives. Break up potatoes into chunks.   *Makes 8 servings*

Prep Time: 10 minutes • **Cook Time:** 7 to 9 hours (LOW) or 4 to 6 hours (HIGH)

Homestead Succotash

    ¼ pound bacon, diced
    1 cup chopped onion
    ½ teaspoon dried thyme leaves
    1 can (15¼ ounces) DEL MONTE® Whole Kernel Golden Sweet Corn,
        drained
    1 can (15¼ ounces) DEL MONTE Green Lima Beans, drained

1. Cook bacon in skillet until crisp; drain. Add onion and thyme; cook until onion is tender.

2. Stir in vegetables and heat through.   *Makes 6 to 8 servings*

Microwave Directions: In shallow 1-quart microwavable dish, cook bacon on HIGH 6 minutes or until crisp; drain. Add onion and thyme; cover and cook on HIGH 2 to 3 minutes or until onion is tender. Add vegetables. Cover and cook on HIGH 3 to 4 minutes or until heated through.

Prep and Cook Time: 13 minutes

Chunky Ranch Potatoes

Glazed Parsnips and Carrots

1 pound parsnips
1 package (8 ounces) baby carrots
1 tablespoon canola oil
    Salt and black pepper
¼ cup orange juice
1 tablespoon butter
1 tablespoon honey
⅛ teaspoon ground ginger

1. Preheat oven to 425°F. Peel parsnips; cut into wedges to match size of baby carrots.

2. Spread vegetables in shallow roasting pan. Drizzle with oil and season with salt and pepper; toss to coat. Bake 30 to 35 minutes or until fork-tender.

3. Combine orange juice, butter, honey and ginger in large skillet. Add vegetables; cook and stir over high heat 1 to 2 minutes or until glazed.   *Makes 6 servings*

Spinach Pie

1 tablespoon FILIPPO BERIO® Olive Oil
1 pound fresh spinach, washed, drained and stems removed
1 medium potato, cooked and mashed
2 eggs, beaten
¼ cup cottage cheese
2 tablespoons grated Romano cheese
    Salt

Preheat oven to 350°F. Grease 8-inch round cake pan with olive oil. Tear spinach into bite-size pieces. In large bowl, combine spinach, potato, eggs, cottage cheese and Romano cheese. Spoon mixture into prepared pan. Bake 15 to 20 minutes or until set. Season to taste with salt.   *Makes 6 servings*

Glazed Parsnips and Carrots

Honey-Lemon Green and Yellow Beans

2½ quarts water
1 pound green beans
1 pound yellow wax beans
2 tablespoons butter
2 tablespoons honey
1 tablespoon grated lemon peel
Salt and black pepper

1. Bring water to a boil in large saucepan. Add beans; boil 2 minutes. Transfer immediately to bowl of ice water. Drain and pat dry.*

2. Melt butter in large nonstick skillet over medium-high heat. Add beans; cook and stir 2 minutes or until heated through. Add honey; cook 1 minute. Remove from heat; stir in lemon peel. Season with salt and pepper. Serve immediately.

Makes 8 servings

This can be done several hours ahead. Cover and refrigerate beans until ready to use.

Saucy Asparagus Casserole

2 pounds asparagus, trimmed
1 can (10¾ ounces) CAMPBELL'S® Condensed Cream of Asparagus Soup
⅓ cup milk or water
½ cup dry bread crumbs
2 tablespoons butter, melted

1. Place the asparagus in a 13×9×2-inch (3-quart) shallow baking dish.

2. Stir the soup and milk in a small bowl and pour over the asparagus. Mix the bread crumbs with the butter in a small bowl and sprinkle over the soup mixture.

3. Bake at 400°F for 20 minutes or until golden brown and bubbly.

Makes 6 servings

Prep Time: 5 minutes • **Bake Time:** 20 minutes

Honey-Lemon Green and Yellow Beans

Creamy Red Potato Salad

3 pounds red bliss or new potatoes, cut into ¾-inch chunks
½ cup WISH-BONE® Italian Dressing*
¾ cup HELLMANN'S® or BEST FOODS® Real Mayonnaise
½ cup sliced green onions
1 teaspoon Dijon mustard
1 teaspoon lemon juice
⅛ teaspoon ground black pepper

*Also terrific with WISH-BONE® Robusto Italian or House Italian Dressing.

1. Cover potatoes with water in 4-quart saucepot; bring to a boil over medium-high heat. Reduce heat to low and simmer 10 minutes or until potatoes are tender. Drain and cool slightly.

2. Combine all ingredients except potatoes in large salad bowl. Add potatoes and toss gently. Serve chilled or at room temperature. *Makes 10 servings*

Fresh Limas in Onion Cream

1 pound fresh lima beans *or* 1 (10-ounce) package frozen lima beans, thawed
⅔ cup milk
½ teaspoon dried minced onion
1 tablespoon butter
1 onion, sliced into rings
⅓ cup sour cream
2 teaspoons sliced pimiento
Salt and black pepper

1. To shell beans, open pods at seams by pinching pods between thumbs and forefingers. Remove beans; discard shells.

2. Place beans in small heavy saucepan; add milk and minced onion. Bring to a boil over medium heat. Reduce heat to low; simmer 20 to 25 minutes or until tender.

3. Meanwhile, heat butter in small skillet over medium-high heat until melted and bubbly. Add onion rings; cook and stir until golden brown. Transfer to lima bean mixture. Stir in sour cream and pimiento. Season with salt and pepper. Serve immediately. *Makes 4 servings*

Creamy Red Potato Salad

Simple Herbed Broccoli

1¼ pounds broccoli
1 quart water
2 tablespoons lemon juice
1 teaspoon extra-virgin olive oil
1 clove garlic, minced
1 teaspoon chopped fresh Italian parsley
Dash black pepper

1. Trim broccoli, discarding tough stems. Cut broccoli into florets with 2-inch stems. Peel remaining broccoli stems; cut into ½-inch-thick slices.

2. Bring water to a boil in large saucepan over high heat. Add broccoli; return to a boil. Reduce heat to medium-high. Cook 3 to 5 minutes or until tender. Drain; transfer to serving dish.

3. Combine lemon juice, oil, garlic, parsley and pepper in small bowl. Pour over broccoli; toss to coat. Cover and let stand 1 hour before serving to allow flavors to blend. Serve at room temperature. *Makes 4 servings*

Mashed Maple Sweet Potatoes

3 cans (15 ounces each) PRINCELLA® or SUGARY SAM® Cut Sweet
    Potatoes, drained
4 tablespoons butter
¼ cup half-and-half
3 tablespoons maple syrup
    Salt and black pepper to taste

Preheat oven to 350°F. In medium mixing bowl, combine all ingredients; beat with an electric mixer on medium speed until well blended. Transfer mixture to a greased 9-inch square casserole dish; smooth the surface. Cover and bake for 30 minutes.
Makes 5 to 7 servings

Simple Herbed Broccoli

Cauliflower Gratin

Vegetable cooking spray
1 can (10¾ ounces) CAMPBELL'S® Condensed Cream of Mushroom Soup
    (Regular or 98% Fat Free)
½ cup milk
1 clove garlic, minced
1 bag (20 ounces) frozen cauliflower flowerets, thawed (about 5 cups)
1 cup finely grated Swiss cheese (about 4 ounces)
¼ cup cooked crumbled bacon or real bacon bits

1. Spray an 11×8-inch (2 quart) shallow baking dish with cooking spray. Stir the soup, milk, garlic, cauliflower, and ½ **cup** of the cheese in the casserole. Sprinkle with the bacon and remaining cheese.

2. Bake at 350°F. for 50 minutes or until the cauliflower is tender and mixture is hot and bubbly. *Makes 6 servings*

Prep Time: 10 minutes • **Bake Time:** 50 minutes

Red Cabbage with Apples

1 head red cabbage, shredded
2 apples, cored, peeled and thinly sliced
½ cup sliced onion
½ cup unsweetened apple juice
¼ cup lemon juice
2 tablespoons raisins
2 tablespoons brown sugar
Salt and black pepper

Combine cabbage, apples, onion, apple juice, lemon juice, raisins and brown sugar in large nonstick saucepan. Cover and simmer over medium-low heat 30 minutes or until tender. Season with salt and pepper. *Makes 8 servings*

Cauliflower Gratin

New Potatoes and Peas

9 small new potatoes, cut into quarters (about 1½ pounds)
1 can (10¾ ounces) CAMPBELL'S® Condensed Cream of Mushroom Soup (Regular or 98% Fat Free)
⅓ cup milk
½ teaspoon dried thyme leaves or dill weed, crushed
⅛ teaspoon ground black pepper
1 package (10 ounces) frozen peas or peas with pearl onions, thawed and drained

1. Place the potatoes in a 4-quart saucepan. Cover the potatoes with water. Heat over high heat to a boil. Reduce the heat to medium. Cook for 8 minutes or until the potatoes are fork-tender. Drain the potatoes in a colander.

2. In the same saucepan, stir the soup, milk, thyme and black pepper. Stir in the potatoes and peas. Heat over low heat, stirring occasionally until heated through.

Makes 7 servings

Prep Time: 10 minutes • **Cook Time:** 20 minutes

Beets in Spicy Mustard Sauce

3 pounds beets, trimmed
¼ cup sour cream
2 tablespoons spicy brown mustard
2 teaspoons lemon juice
2 cloves garlic, minced
⅛ teaspoon dried thyme
¼ teaspoon black pepper

1. Place beets in large saucepan; add enough water to cover by 1 inch. Bring to a boil over medium-high heat. Reduce heat to medium-low; cover and simmer 25 minutes or until beets are tender. Drain well. Peel beets; cut into ¼-inch-thick slices.

2. Combine sour cream, mustard, lemon juice, garlic, thyme and pepper in small saucepan; cook and stir over medium heat until heated through. Spoon sauce over beets; toss gently to coat.

Makes 4 servings

New Potatoes and Peas

Sweet Treats

Spicy Butterscotch Snack Cake

1 cup (2 sticks) butter or margarine, softened
1 cup sugar
2 eggs
½ teaspoon vanilla extract
½ cup applesauce
2½ cups all-purpose flour
1½ to 2 teaspoons ground cinnamon
1 teaspoon baking soda
½ teaspoon salt
1¾ cups (11-ounce package) HERSHEY'S Butterscotch Chips
1 cup chopped pecans (optional)
Powdered sugar or frozen whipped topping, thawed (optional)

1. Heat oven to 350°F. Lightly grease 13×9×2-inch baking pan.

2. Beat butter and sugar in large bowl until fluffy. Add eggs and vanilla; beat well. Mix in applesauce. Stir together flour, cinnamon, baking soda and salt; gradually add to butter mixture, beating until well blended. Stir in butterscotch chips and pecans, if desired. Spread in prepared pan.

3. Bake 35 to 40 minutes or until wooden pick inserted in center comes out clean. Cool completely in pan on wire rack. Dust with powdered sugar or serve with whipped topping, if desired. *Makes 12 to 16 servings*

Deep-Dish Blueberry Pie

    Pie Dough for 2-Crust Pie (recipe follows)
    6 cups fresh blueberries *or* 2 (16 ounce) packages frozen blueberries, thawed
    2 tablespoons lemon juice
1¼ cups sugar
    3 tablespoons quick-cooking tapioca
    ¼ teaspoon ground cinnamon
    1 tablespoon butter, cubed

1. Prepare Pie Dough for a 2-Crust Pie. Preheat oven to 400°F.

2. Place blueberries in large bowl and sprinkle with lemon juice. Combine sugar, tapioca and cinnamon in small bowl; gently stir into blueberries until blended.

3. Roll 1 disc dough into 12-inch circle on lightly floured work surface. Fit dough into 9-inch deep-dish pie pan. Trim all but ½ inch of overhang. Pour blueberry mixture into pan; dot top with butter pieces.

4. Roll remaining disc dough into 10-inch circle. Using small cookie cutter or knife, cut 4 or 5 shapes from dough for vents. Lift and center dough over blueberry mixture in pie pan. Trim dough, leaving 1-inch border. Fold excess dough under and even with pan edge. Crimp edges with fork tines.

5. Bake 15 minutes. *Reduce oven temperature to 350°F.* Bake 40 minutes or until crust is golden brown. Cool on wire rack 30 minutes before serving.   *Makes 9 servings*

Pie Dough for a 2-Crust Pie

    2½ cups all-purpose flour
      1 teaspoon *each* salt and sugar
      1 cup (2 sticks) cold unsalted butter, cubed
    ⅓ cup cold water

1. Combine flour, salt and sugar in large bowl. Cut in butter using pastry blender or 2 knives until mixture resembles coarse crumbs.

2. Drizzle 2 tablespoons water over mixture; stir to blend. Repeat with remaining water. Knead dough just until it comes together. Divide dough in half. Shape each half into disc; wrap in plastic wrap. Refrigerate at least 1 hour.

Makes dough for 2-crust pie

Deep-Dish Blueberry Pie

Grandma's Favorite Sugarcakes

⅔ cup butter or margarine, softened
1½ cups packed light brown sugar
1 cup granulated sugar
2 eggs
2 teaspoons vanilla extract
4½ cups all-purpose flour
2 teaspoons baking soda
1 teaspoon baking powder
1 teaspoon salt
1 cup buttermilk or sour milk*
2 cups (12-ounce package) HERSHEY'S Mini Chips Semi-Sweet Chocolate
2 cups chopped walnuts or pecans
Vanilla frosting (optional)
Colored sugar or sprinkles (optional)

*To sour milk, use 1 tablespoon white vinegar plus milk to equal 1 cup.

1. Heat oven to 350°F. Grease cookie sheet.

2. Beat butter, brown sugar and granulated sugar until well blended in large mixing bowl. Add eggs and vanilla; beat until creamy. Stir together flour, baking soda, baking powder and salt; add alternately with buttermilk to butter mixture, beating well after each addition. Stir in small chocolate chips and nuts. Drop by level ¼ cups or heaping tablespoons 2 inches apart onto prepared cookie sheet.

3. Bake 12 to 14 minutes or until golden brown. Cool slightly; remove to wire rack. Cool completely. Frost with favorite vanilla frosting; garnish with colored sugar, if desired.

Makes 3 dozen cookies

Grandma's Favorite Sugarcakes

Cinnamon Pear Crisp

    8 pears, peeled and sliced
    ¾ cup unsweetened apple juice concentrate
    ½ cup golden raisins
    ¼ cup plus 3 tablespoons all-purpose flour, divided
    1 teaspoon ground cinnamon
    ⅓ cup quick oats
    3 tablespoons packed dark brown sugar
    3 tablespoons butter, melted

1. Preheat oven to 375°F. Coat 11×7-inch baking dish with nonstick cooking spray.

2. Combine pears, apple juice concentrate, raisins, 3 tablespoons flour and cinnamon in large bowl; mix well. Transfer to prepared baking dish.

3. Combine oats, remaining ¼ cup flour, brown sugar and butter in medium bowl; stir until mixture resembles coarse crumbs. Sprinkle evenly over pear mixture. Bake 1 hour or until golden brown. Cool in pan on wire rack.

Makes 8 to 10 servings

Raisin Apple Bread Pudding

    4 cups white bread cubes
    1 medium apple, chopped
    1 cup raisins
    2 large eggs
    1 can (12 fluid ounces) NESTLÉ® CARNATION® Evaporated Milk
    ½ cup apple juice
    ½ cup granulated sugar
1½ teaspoons ground cinnamon
    1 jar caramel ice cream topping (optional)

PREHEAT oven to 350°F. Grease 11×7-inch baking dish.

COMBINE bread, apple and raisins in large bowl. Beat eggs in medium bowl. Stir in evaporated milk, apple juice, sugar and cinnamon; mix well. Pour egg mixture over bread mixture, pressing bread into milk mixture; let stand for 10 minutes. Pour into prepared baking dish.

BAKE for 40 to 45 minutes or until set and apples are tender. Serve warm with caramel topping.

Makes 8 servings

Cinnamon Pear Crisp

Lattice-Topped Deep-Dish Cherry Pie

2 cans (about 14 ounces each) pitted tart red cherries in water
½ cup sugar
3 tablespoons quick-cooking tapioca
¼ teaspoon almond extract
¾ cup all-purpose flour
¼ teaspoon salt
3 tablespoons shortening
2 to 3 tablespoons cold water

1. Preheat oven to 375°F. Drain 1 can cherries. Combine drained cherries, remaining can cherries with juice, sugar, tapioca and almond extract in large bowl.

2. Combine flour and salt in small bowl. Cut in shortening with pastry blender or 2 knives until mixture resembles coarse crumbs. Add water, 1 tablespoon at a time, stirring just until moistened. Form dough into ball. Roll dough into 9×8-inch rectangle on lightly floured surface. Cut into 9 (8×1-inch) strips.

3. Spoon cherry mixture into 13×9-inch baking dish. Place 4 dough strips diagonally over cherry mixture. Weave remaining 5 dough strips diagonally across. Pinch strips at ends to seal.

4. Bake 40 to 50 minutes or until filling is bubbling and crust is golden brown. Remove to wire rack; cool slightly before serving. Serve in bowls.

Makes 9 servings

Prep Time: 15 minutes • **Bake Time:** 40 to 50 minutes

Lattice-Topped Deep-Dish Cherry Pie

Rustic Fall Fruit Tart

1½ cups all-purpose flour
½ cup (1 stick) butter, softened
½ cup (½ of 8-ounce container) PHILADELPHIA® Cream Cheese Spread
4 medium plums, thinly sliced
2 medium nectarines, thinly sliced
½ cup sugar
1 teaspoon ground ginger
1 tablespoon cornstarch
⅓ cup apricot jam

1. Place flour, butter and cream cheese in food processor container; cover. Process, using pulsing action, until mixture is well blended and almost forms a ball. Shape dough into ball; wrap tightly with plastic wrap. Refrigerate 1 hour or until chilled.

2. Preheat oven to 400°F. Place pastry on lightly floured surface; roll out to 12-inch circle. Place on lightly greased baking sheet; set aside. Toss fruit with sugar, ginger and cornstarch. Arrange decoratively over crust to within 2 inches of edge of crust. Fold edge of crust over fruit.

3. Bake 30 minutes. Remove from oven; spread fruit with jam. Serve warm or at room temperature. *Makes 8 servings*

Prep Time: 15 minutes • **Bake Time:** 30 minutes

Vanilla Rice Pudding

3 cups milk, divided
1 cup MINUTE® White Rice, uncooked
⅓ cup raisins (optional)
1 package (4-serving size) vanilla-flavor instant pudding and pie filling

Bring 1 cup milk to a boil in medium saucepan. Stir in rice and raisins, if desired; cover. Remove from heat. Let stand 5 minutes.

Prepare pudding as directed on package in large bowl with remaining 2 cups milk.

Add rice mixture to prepared pudding; mix well. Cover surface of pudding with plastic wrap; cool 5 minutes. Serve warm or chilled. *Makes 6 servings*

Rustic Fall Fruit Tart

Brown Sugar Spice Cake

    Vegetable cooking spray
1 can (10¾ ounces) CAMPBELL'S® Condensed Tomato Soup
    (Regular or Healthy Request®)
½ cup water
2 eggs
1 box (about 18 ounces) spice cake mix
1¼ cups hot water
¾ cup packed brown sugar
1 teaspoon ground cinnamon
    Vanilla ice cream

Slow Cooker Directions

1. Spray the inside of a 4-quart slow cooker with the cooking spray.

2. Combine the soup, water, eggs and cake mix in a medium bowl and mix according to the package directions. Pour the batter into the cooker.

3. Stir the water, brown sugar and cinnamon in a small bowl. Pour over the batter.

4. Cover and cook on HIGH for 2 hours or until a knife inserted in the center comes out clean.

5. Spoon the cake into bowls, spooning the sauce from the bottom of the cooker. Serve warm with the ice cream. *Makes 8 servings*

Kitchen Tip: This warm, gooey dessert would be great sprinkled with crunchy candied walnuts.

Prep Time: 10 minutes • **Cook Time:** 2 hours

Brown Sugar Spice Cake

Classic Apple Pie

    1 package (15 ounces) refrigerated pie crusts
    6 cups sliced Granny Smith apples (about 6 medium)
    ½ cup sugar
    1 tablespoon cornstarch
    2 teaspoons lemon juice
    ½ teaspoon ground cinnamon
    ½ teaspoon vanilla
    ⅛ teaspoon *each* salt, ground nutmeg and ground cloves
    1 tablespoon whipping cream

1. Preheat oven to 350°F. Line 9-inch pie pan with 1 pie crust. (Refrigerate remaining pie crust while preparing apples.)

2. Combine apples, sugar, cornstarch, lemon juice, cinnamon, vanilla, salt, nutmeg and cloves in large bowl; mix well. Pour into prepared crust. Place second crust over apples; crimp edge to seal.

3. Cut 4 slits in top crust; brush with cream. Bake 40 minutes or until crust is golden brown. Cool slightly before serving.   *Makes 8 servings*

Sour Cream Squash Pie

    1 package (12 ounces) frozen winter squash, thawed and drained
    ½ cup sour cream
    ¼ cup sugar
    1 egg
  1½ teaspoons pumpkin pie spice
    ½ teaspoon salt
    ½ teaspoon vanilla
    ¾ cup evaporated milk
    1 (9-inch) graham cracker pie crust
    ¼ cup chopped hazelnuts, toasted

1. Preheat oven to 350°F. Whisk squash, sour cream, sugar, egg, pumpkin pie spice, salt and vanilla in large bowl until blended. Whisk in milk. Pour into crust.

2. Bake 1 hour and 10 minutes or until set. Cool completely; sprinkle with hazelnuts just before serving.   *Makes 8 servings*

Classic Apple Pie

Autumn Fruit Cobbler

3 large apples, cored and cut into ¼-inch wedges
2 medium-firm ripe Bartlett or Bosc pears, peeled, quartered and cored
⅓ cup dried cranberries
1 cup packed light brown sugar, divided
2 tablespoons cornstarch
1½ teaspoons ground cinnamon, divided
1½ cups all-purpose flour
1 cup QUAKER® Oats (quick or old fashioned, uncooked)
2 teaspoons baking powder
¼ teaspoon salt
½ cup (1 stick) margarine or butter, chilled
⅔ cup low-fat (2%) milk
Vanilla ice cream (optional)

1. Heat oven to 400°F. Combine apples, pears and cranberries in large bowl. Combine ¾ cup brown sugar, cornstarch and 1 teaspoon cinnamon in small bowl; mix well. Add to fruit; mix well. Spoon into 2½-quart glass baking dish. Bake, uncovered, 30 minutes.

2. Combine flour, oats, remaining ¼ cup brown sugar, baking powder, salt and remaining ½ teaspoon cinnamon in large bowl; mix well. Cut in margarine with pastry blender or 2 knives until mixture resembles coarse crumbs. Add milk; mix with fork until soft dough forms. Turn out onto lightly floured surface; knead gently 6 to 8 times. Pat dough into ½-inch-thick rectangle. Cut with floured biscuit or cookie cutter.

3. Remove baking dish from oven; stir fruit. Carefully arrange biscuits over hot fruit; press lightly into fruit. Bake 15 to 20 minutes or until biscuits are golden brown and fruit mixture is bubbly. Serve warm with vanilla ice cream, if desired. Cover and refrigerate leftovers. *Makes 8 servings*

Autumn Fruit Cobbler

Acknowledgments

The publisher would like to thank the companies and organizations listed below for the use of their recipes and photographs in this publication.

Allens®

The Beef Checkoff

Bob Evans®

Cabot® Creamery Cooperative

Campbell Soup Company

Cream of Wheat® Cereal

Del Monte Foods

Filippo Berio® Olive Oil

The Hershey Company

Hormel Foods, LLC

Kraft Foods Global, Inc.

Michael Foods, Inc.

Nestlé USA

North Dakota Wheat Commission

The Quaker® Oatmeal Kitchens

Riviana Foods Inc.

Tyson Foods, Inc.

Unilever

US Dry Bean Council

Index

Index